The Little
SALAD
Cookbook

THE LITTLE
SALAD
COOKBOOK

ACROPOLIS BOOKS

First published by Ultimate Editions in 1996

© 1996 Anness Publishing Limited

Ultimate Editions is an imprint of
Anness Publishing Limited
1 Boundary Row
London SE1 8HP

This edition distributed in Canada by
Book Express, an imprint of
Raincoast Books Distribution Limited

ISBN 1 86035 101 8

Publisher Joanna Lorenz
Senior Cookery Editor Linda Fraser
Assistant Editor Emma Brown
Designers Patrick McLeavey & Jo Brewer
Illustrator Anna Koska
Photographers Karl Adamson, Michael Michaels,
James Duncan, Steve Baxter, Amanda Heywood &
Edward Allwright
Recipes Christine France, Roz Denny, Catherine
Atkinson, Hilaire Walden, Steven Wheeler, Annie
Nichols, Shirley Gill & Norma MacMillan

For all recipes, quantities are given in both metric and
imperial measures, and, where appropriate, measures are
also given in standard cups and spoons. Follow one set, but
not a mixture, because they are not interchangeable.

Printed in Singapore by
Star Standard Industries Pte Ltd

Contents

Introduction

Thanks to the abundance of good quality salad-stuffs in our supermarkets, these once seasonal treats can now be enjoyed every day. It is true that there's a special pleasure in gathering greens and fresh herbs from the garden, but when summer gives way to autumn, and even the cut-and-come again lettuces no longer yield fresh young leaves, it is satisfying to know that salads can still be on the menu.

There's no better way to exercise artistic flair than in assembling a salad. Even a simple green salad can offer subtle variations in shape, texture, colour and flavour. Contrast a crisp iceberg lettuce with a soft butterhead; the pale leaves of lollo biondo with the matt glossy green of watercress. Balance bland flavours with a few leaves of bitter escarole, or introduce an underlying lemon flavour with some shreds of sorrel. Nasturtium leaves add a peppery tang, as does rocket, while young spinach leaves are valued for their rich sweetness. For extra colour, choose the red or purple hues of oakleaf, lollo rosso or red cabbage, perhaps accentuated by a few feathery leaves from the heart of a frisée lettuce. Take care not to overdo it; two or three different types of leaf, chosen for their complementary or contrasting qualities, will be more effective than an ill-assorted medley.

As for extra ingredients, the list is almost endless. Salad vegetables include avocados, artichokes, asparagus, green beans, carrots, cauliflower florets, celery, cucumber, fennel, peppers of every colour, radishes and onions, especially Spanish or mild red onions. Tomatoes too, although these are often served on their own, with a simple olive oil dressing and snippings of basil. Vinegar is seldom added because tomatoes are themselves acidic. Fruits, especially oranges, apples, pears, grapes and melons, frequently feature in salads.

Potato salads are in a category of their own, and there are also many hearty salads based on rice, pasta or grains, including the famous tabbouleh. Meats, fish and shellfish make a major contribution.

In a formal meal, it is traditional to serve a simple salad after the entrée, to cleanse the palate before dessert, but a salad can serve equally well as a starter, accompaniment or substantial main course.

Salads were originally seasoned solely with salt (hence the name) but are now inseparably associated with a whole host of dressings, from simple mixtures of oil and vinegar or lemon juice to sauces based on mayonnaise, yogurt or blue cheese. Hot dressings, often with a foundation of bacon fat (the crisp fried bacon giving the salad extra flavour and texture) are increasingly popular, but must be added only at the last minute; if either dinner or diner is late, the leaves will become limp and the salad will be spoiled.

We are constantly being encouraged to eat more fresh vegetables and fruit. What better way to enjoy these ingredients than in a salad that is as pleasing to look at and to make as it is delicious to eat?

Familiar Salad Leaves

BUTTERHEAD LETTUCE

Also known as cabbage lettuce, because of its shape, this has soft leaves with a slightly buttery taste.

CHINESE LEAF

Two types of this crunchy vegetable are commonly seen; one is longer and more pointed than the other. Both have delicately flavoured long, crinkly leaves with crisp, white stems. It is available all year round and keeps well in the fridge.

COS LETTUCE

Firm, tapering leaves with a stiff central rib, tightly packed to form an elongated head, the cos or romaine lettuce is one of the most familiar and most widely available salad vegetables.

ENDIVE

There are several varieties of this loose-leaved salad vegetable: Batavian endive (escarole) has broad, ragged leaves, while the leaves of curly endive (frisée) are frilly, almost spiky. A red broad-leafed variety, radicchio, is favoured for its colour and texture. All endives tend to be rather bitter.

ICEBERG LETTUCE

With its large, firm head and tightly packed, crisp leaves, this is one of the most popular varieties of lettuce. It keeps for longer than most lettuces.

LAMB'S LETTUCE

Also known as corn salad or mâche, lamb's lettuce consists of small smooth green leaves in clusters. The leaves have a mild, sweet flavour. It is preferable to buy lamb's lettuce loose in whole plants, since it is fragile and bruises easily.

LITTLE GEM

Resembling a miniature cos lettuce, the Little Gem has neat well-formed oval leaves with a slightly nutty flavour.

LOLLO BIONDO/LOLLO ROSSO

Mild-tasting lollo lettuces have distinctive, frilly leaves forming a loose head. Lollo biondo is pale and creamy; rosso has leaves tinged with dark red.

OAKLEAF LETTUCE

Also known as feuille de chêne and red salad bowl, this lettuce is favoured for its colour (bronze to purple) and its delicate flavour. It has loose leaves branching from a single stalk.

ROCKET

This easy-to-grow, old-fashioned salad herb rewards gardeners with irregular, small, dark leaves which have a peppery flavour with a hint of citrus.

SALAD CRESS

Cress is bought growing in small trays or boxes; one simply snips off what is needed. It is a popular and pretty salad ingredient.

SORREL

The soft, spade-shaped leaves of this herb have a delicate lemony taste. Use raw sorrel sparingly. It does not keep well and must be bought very fresh.

SPINACH

Tender young spinach leaves have a sweet flavour and are delicious with bacon.

WATERCRESS

Watercress leaves are dark and glossy and grow on sprigged stems. Watercress is a member of the mustard family, as one might suppose from its peppery flavour.

9

Techniques

CHOOSING SALAD LEAVES

For the best flavour and texture, salad leaves must be fresh. Reject any that are wilted or discoloured. Buy or pick only what you can use within the next day or two, and store them in the fridge.

PREPARING SALAD LEAVES

To prepare lettuces, remove the coarse outer leaves, separate the remaining leaves and wash them well. Take care to remove any grit, but do not leave them to soak. Drain well, break off any tough ribs and dry the leaves. Use a salad spinner for the more robust leaves; blot delicate leaves with kitchen paper or a clean absorbent towel. If you must prepare lettuces ahead of time, pack the leaves into polythene bags, close tightly and store in the fridge.

MAKING A SIMPLE DRESSING

Dressings should be carefully chosen in order to complement the ingredients, and should not dominate the salad. A wide range of recipes appears in this collection, but for a simple French dressing the rule of thumb is to use three parts of olive oil to one part of wine vinegar, adding a pinch each of caster sugar, salt and pepper, and mustard powder or made mustard, for flavouring. Either combine all the ingredients in a screw-top jar, close tightly and shake well, or mix together the vinegar and the flavourings, then whisk in the oil.

TOSSING A GREEN SALAD

Rub the inside of the salad bowl with a cut clove of garlic, if you like. Just before serving, toss the leaves with just enough dressing to coat them. It is better to err on the mean side than to swamp the salad.

TOPPINGS
• Crumbled crisp bacon or toasted nori (dried seaweed)
• Toasted sunflower, sesame or pumpkin seeds
• Snipped chives, chopped parsley or other fresh herbs
• Grated hard-boiled egg (white and yolk)
• Grated cheese
• Slivers of sun-dried tomato
• Cubes of feta cheese or smoked tofu

SPROUTING BEANS

Beansprouts make a nutritious addition to a salad. Put the dried beans, seeds or grains (try mung beans, aduki beans or alfalfa seeds) in a large glass jar, filling it less than one-sixth full. Cover with muslin or cheesecloth secured by a rubber band, and fill the jar with cold water. Pour the water off and put the jar in a warm, dark spot. Rinse and drain daily. The sprouts will be ready to harvest in 3–6 days, and should be rinsed and drained before use.

COOK'S TIP

The best way to prepare an iceberg lettuce is to remove the core, then hold the head under the tap and run cold water into the cavity. This will gently force the leaves apart, making it easy to remove as many as you need. Discard any outer leaves that have been damaged.

Starters &
Light Meals

Minted Melon Salad

INGREDIENTS

1 ripe orange-fleshed melon
1 ripe green or white-fleshed melon
mint sprigs, to garnish
DRESSING
30ml/2 tbsp roughly chopped fresh mint
5ml/1 tsp caster sugar
30ml/2 tbsp raspberry vinegar
90ml/6 tbsp extra virgin olive oil
salt and ground black pepper

SERVES 6

1 Cut the melons in half, then scoop out and discard the seeds. Using a sharp knife, cut the melons into thin slices. Carefully remove the skins. Take six individual salad plates and arrange slices of the two varieties of melon decoratively on each one.

2 Make the dressing. Mix together the mint, sugar and raspberry vinegar in a small bowl. Gradually whisk in the oil, then add salt and pepper to taste. Alternatively, mix all the ingredients in a screw-top jar, close tightly and shake vigorously to combine.

3 Spoon the dressing over the melon slices. Serve lightly chilled and garnished with mint sprigs.

Aubergine & Red Pepper Pâté with Radicchio

INGREDIENTS

1 radicchio lettuce, separated into leaves
1 butterhead lettuce, separated into leaves
crispbreads, to serve
PATE
3 aubergines
2 red peppers
5 garlic cloves
7.5ml / 1 ½ tsp pink peppercorns in brine,
drained and crushed (optional)
30ml / 2 tbsp chopped fresh coriander

SERVES 6

1 Make the pâté. Preheat the oven to 200°C/400°F/ Gas 6. Arrange the whole aubergines, peppers and the unpeeled garlic cloves on a baking sheet. Bake for 10 minutes, then remove the garlic cloves. Turn the vegetables over and bake for 20 minutes more. Peel the garlic and put into a food processor or blender.

2 Remove the charred red peppers from the oven. Place in a plastic bag, close tightly and leave to cool. Bake the aubergines for a further 10 minutes.

3 Remove the aubergines from the oven, split them in half and scoop the flesh into a sieve placed over a bowl. Press the flesh with a spoon to remove the bitter juices, then add to the garlic. Process until smooth, then scrape into a large bowl.

4 Remove the red peppers from the plastic bag and rub or peel off the skins and discard. Remove and discard the seeds, then chop the flesh finely. Stir the diced peppers into the aubergine and garlic mixture together with the pink peppercorns, if using, and the chopped fresh coriander.

5 Choose a few radicchio and butterhead lettuce leaves of similar size and arrange them in an attractive pattern around the edges of six individual salad plates. Place a few spoonfuls of the aubergine and red pepper pâté in the centre of each plate of salad. Serve at once, with crispbreads, if liked.

Melon & Parma Ham Salad

INGREDIENTS

1 large melon (cantaloupe, Galia or Charentais)
175g/6oz Parma or Serrano ham, thinly sliced
SALSA
225g/8oz strawberries, hulled
5ml/1 tsp caster sugar
30ml/2 tbsp groundnut or sunflower oil
15ml/1 tbsp orange juice
2.5ml/½ tsp finely grated orange rind
2.5ml/½ tsp finely grated fresh root ginger
salt and ground black pepper

SERVES 4

1 Cut the melon in half and then scoop out and discard the seeds. Using a sharp knife, cut the melon into thick slices. Carefully remove the skin.

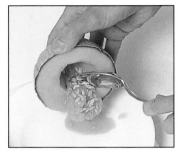

Place the slices on a large plate in a single layer, cover and chill in the fridge until ready to serve.

2 Make the salsa. Cut the strawberries into large dice. Place them in a bowl with the sugar and crush lightly to release the juices. Add the oil, orange juice,

orange rind and ginger. Season with salt and a generous grinding of black pepper.

3 Arrange the melon on a serving plate and drape the ham over the top. Serve with strawberry salsa.

20

Smoked Trout & Horseradish Salad

INGREDIENTS

675g / 1½lb new potatoes, scrubbed
115g / 4oz mixed lettuce leaves
4 smoked trout fillets, skinned and flaked
4 slices of dark rye bread, cut into small fingers
4 cherry tomatoes, halved
salt and ground black pepper
DRESSING
60ml / 4 tbsp creamed horseradish
15ml / 1 tbsp white wine vinegar
60ml / 4 tbsp groundnut oil
10ml / 2 tsp caraway seeds

SERVES 4

1 Place the potatoes in a large pan of salted water. Bring to the boil, lower the heat slightly and cook for 15–20 minutes or until just tender. Drain and cool.

2 Make the dressing. Mix the horseradish and vinegar in a small bowl. Whisk in the oil. Stir in the caraway seeds. Alternatively, mix the ingredients in a screw-top jar, close tightly and shake to combine.

3 Put the prepared salad leaves in a bowl. Season with salt and pepper and toss with a little of the dressing. Cut the potatoes in half. Arrange the trout, potatoes, rye

fingers and cherry tomatoes on the salad, drizzle over a little more dressing and serve. Offer the remaining dressing separately.

Main Course
Salads

New Orleans Steak Salad

INGREDIENTS

4 sirloin or rump steaks, about 175g/6oz each
1 butterhead lettuce, separated into leaves
1 bunch watercress, trimmed
4 tomatoes, quartered
4 drained canned artichoke hearts, halved
175g/6oz button mushrooms, sliced
4 spring onions, sliced
4 large gherkins, sliced
a few green olives
salt and ground black pepper
FRENCH DRESSING
15ml/1 tbsp white wine vinegar
5ml/1 tsp Dijon mustard
pinch of caster sugar
90ml/6 tbsp extra virgin olive oil

SERVES 4

1 Preheat the grill. Season the steaks with black pepper. Place them on a rack over a grill pan and cook for 6–8 minutes, turning once, until they are medium rare. Cover the steaks with domed foil and leave in a warm place while you assemble the rest of the salad.

2 Make the dressing. Mix the vinegar, mustard and sugar in a small bowl, then whisk in the oil. Alternatively, mix all the ingredients in a screw-top jar, close tightly and shake to combine.

3 Put the prepared lettuce, watercress, tomatoes, artichoke hearts and mushrooms in a bowl. Add the dressing and toss together lightly. Divide the salad among four plates and arrange the spring onions, gherkins and olives on each. Slice each steak diagonally and arrange over the salads. Season with salt and pepper and serve at once.

23

Goat's Cheese Salad with Buckwheat, Fresh Figs & Walnuts

INGREDIENTS

175g/6oz/1½ cups couscous
30ml/2 tbsp toasted buckwheat
30ml/2 tbsp chopped fresh parsley
60ml/4 tbsp olive oil
45ml/3 tbsp walnut oil
115g/4oz rocket leaves
½ frisée lettuce, separated into leaves
175g/6oz crumbly white goat's cheese
50g/2oz/½ cup walnut pieces, toasted
4 ripe figs
salt and ground black pepper

SERVES 4

I Mix the couscous and buckwheat together in a heatproof bowl. Pour over enough boiling water to cover and leave to soak for 15 minutes. Drain well in a sieve, then spread the mixture out on a metal tray and set aside to dry out a little more.

2 Tip the couscous mixture into a bowl. Add the chopped fresh parsley. Mix the olive oil and walnut oil together, add half the dressing to the couscous mixture and toss lightly. Season to taste with plenty of salt and ground black pepper

3 Place the prepared rocket and frisée leaves in a separate bowl, add the remaining oil mixture and toss to coat. Arrange the dressed salad leaves on four large plates, especially around the edges, and pile couscous mixture in the centre of each one.

4 Crumble or cube the goat's cheese and arrange it over the salads, then scatter with the toasted walnut pieces. Using a sharp knife, carefully cut each fig into four from the top almost to the base. Leave the quarters joined at the base so that they open out like the petals of a flower. Gently centre a fig on each salad and serve immediately.

24

Grilled Salmon & Spring Vegetable Salad

INGREDIENTS

350g/12oz small new potatoes, scrubbed
4 quail's eggs
115g/4oz baby courgettes, topped and tailed
115g/4oz young carrots, peeled
115g/4oz baby sweetcorn
115g/4oz sugar snap peas, trimmed
115g/4oz fine green beans, trimmed
115g/4oz patty pan squash (optional)
120ml/4fl oz French dressing
4 salmon fillets, about 150g/5oz each, skinned
*115g/4oz sorrel or young spinach, leaves
stripped from stems*
salt and ground black pepper

SERVES 4

1 Put the potatoes in a pan of salted water. Bring to the boil, lower the heat slightly and cook for 15–20 minutes or until just tender. Drain and keep warm.

2 Put the quail's eggs in a pan. Add boiling water to cover and simmer for 7–8 minutes. Cool under cold running water. Shell the eggs and cut them in half.

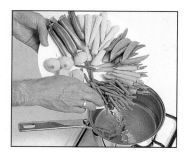

3 Peel the courgettes decoratively. Cook the carrots, sweetcorn, peas, beans, courgettes and squash (if using) in a pan of boiling water for about 2 minutes. Drain well and put in a bowl. Add the potatoes. Toss with a little French dressing, season and allow to cool. Preheat the grill.

4 Put the salmon fillets on a rack over a grill pan, brush with a little of the dressing and grill them for 6 minutes, turning once. Meanwhile, put the sorrel or spinach leaves in a stainless steel or enamel saucepan. Add 60ml/4 tbsp of the dressing, cover and soften over a gentle heat for 2 minutes. Strain the sorrel or spinach and cool to room temperature.

5 Arrange the salmon, spring vegetables and potatoes on four large plates. Place a spoonful of sorrel or spinach on each piece of salmon, top with a halved hard-boiled quail's egg and serve.

Wild Mushroom Salad with Parma Ham

INGREDIENTS

175g / 6oz Parma ham, thickly sliced
40g / 1½ oz / 3 tbsp butter
450g / 1lb wild and cultivated mushrooms
(chanterelles, field blewits, oyster mushrooms,
champignons de Paris), sliced
½ oakleaf lettuce, separated into leaves
½ frisée lettuce, separated into leaves
15ml / 1 tbsp walnut oil
60ml / 4 tbsp brandy
HERB PANCAKES
45ml / 3 tbsp plain flour
75ml / 5 tbsp milk
1 egg plus 1 egg yolk
60ml / 4 tbsp freshly grated Parmesan cheese
45ml / 3 tbsp chopped mixed fresh herbs
salt and ground black pepper

SERVES 4

1 Make the pancakes. Mix the flour and milk in a measuring jug. Beat in the egg, egg yolk, Parmesan and herbs. Add salt and pepper to taste. Place a lightly greased frying pan over a steady heat. Pour in enough mixture to coat the bottom of the pan.

2 When the batter has set, flip the pancake over and cook the other side, then turn out. Cook more pancakes in the same way. When the pancakes are cool, roll them up together and slice into ribbons.

3 Cut the ham into strips to match the pancake ribbons and toss them lightly together in a bowl. Heat the butter in the clean frying pan. Add the mushrooms and cook for 6–8 minutes.

4 Meanwhile dress the prepared salad leaves with walnut oil. Divide them among four large plates and arrange the ham and pancake ribbons in the centre of each one. Add the brandy to the mushrooms and ignite it. As soon as the flames die down, spoon the mushrooms over the salads. Season with salt and pepper, and serve.

33

Warm Duck Salad with Orange & Coriander

INGREDIENTS

1 small orange
2 boned duck breasts
150ml/¼ pint/⅔ cup dry white wine
5ml/1 tsp ground coriander
2.5ml/½ tsp ground cumin
30ml/2 tbsp caster sugar
juice of ½ lime or small lemon
½ escarole lettuce, separated into leaves
½ frisée lettuce, separated into leaves
30ml/2 tbsp sunflower oil
salt and cayenne pepper
4 coriander sprigs, to garnish
GARLIC CROUTONS
1 garlic clove
45ml/3 tbsp olive oil
75g/3oz thickly sliced day-old bread,
cut into short fingers

SERVES 4

1 Cut the orange in half, then into thick slices. Discard any pips and place the slices in a small saucepan. Add water to cover, heat to simmering and cook for 5 minutes. Drain and set aside.

2 Prick the skin on the duck breasts, then rub the skin with salt. Heat a heavy-based frying pan, add the duck breasts and cook for 20 minutes, turning once, until they are medium-rare.

3 Transfer the duck breasts to a heated plate, cover and keep hot. Pour off the fat from the pan, leaving the sediment behind.

4 Add the wine, spices and sugar to the frying pan and stir over the heat, taking care to incorporate the sediment. Add the orange slices. Boil quickly until the sauce coats the oranges, then sharpen with the lime or lemon juice. Add salt and cayenne to taste and keep warm over a low heat.

5 Make the croûtons in a second frying pan. Peel and bruise the garlic clove. Heat the olive oil with the garlic and when the garlic turns a deep golden brown, remove it with a slotted spoon. Add the bread fingers to the pan and fry until golden brown. Remove and drain on kitchen paper.

6 Sprinkle the prepared lettuce leaves with the sunflower oil and arrange on four large plates. Cut the duck breasts into thick slices diagonally. Using  the composition illustrated opposite, or one of your own, add the duck and glazed orange slices to the plates. Scatter with the croûtons, garnish each salad with a coriander sprig and serve.

Spinach & Bacon Salad

INGREDIENTS

450g/1lb young spinach, leaves stripped
from stems
60ml/4 tbsp red wine vinegar
60ml/4 tbsp water
20ml/4 tsp caster sugar
5ml/1 tsp dry mustard
25ml/1½ tbsp sunflower oil
225g/8oz rindless streaky bacon rashers
8 spring onions, thinly sliced
6 radishes, thinly sliced
2 hard-boiled eggs, coarsely grated
salt and ground black pepper

SERVES 6

1 Put the prepared spinach leaves in a large salad bowl. Mix the vinegar, water, sugar and dry mustard in a separate bowl. Add a pinch of salt and a grinding of black pepper.

2 Heat the oil in a frying pan, add the bacon rashers and fry until very crisp and brown. Remove them with tongs and drain them well on kitchen paper.

3 Add the vinegar mixture to the bacon fat remaining in the pan. Bring to the boil, stirring constantly to incorporate any sediment on the base of the pan. Immediately pour the hot dressing over the spinach salad. Toss quickly to coat the leaves well.

4 Chop the bacon roughly and add it to the spinach. Add the spring onions and radishes and mix gently. Scatter the grated hard-boiled egg over the salad, season to taste and serve at once.

Side Salads

Lettuce & Herb Salad

INGREDIENTS

½ cucumber
mixed salad leaves
1 bunch watercress, trimmed
1 head chicory, sliced
45ml/3 tbsp chopped mixed fresh herbs
(parsley, thyme, mint, tarragon and chives)
DRESSING
15ml/1 tbsp wine vinegar
5ml/1 tsp prepared mustard
75ml/5 tbsp olive oil
salt and ground black pepper

SERVES 4

1 Make the dressing. Put the wine vinegar and mustard in a small bowl and mix together. Whisk in the olive oil gradually and then add salt and pepper to taste. Alternatively, mix all the ingredients in a screw-top jar, close tightly and shake to combine.

2 Peel the cucumber, if liked, then halve it lengthways and scoop out the seeds. Thinly slice the flesh. Tear the prepared mixed salad leaves into bite-size pieces.

3 Mix together the cucumber, salad leaves, watercress, chicory and fresh herbs in a large bowl. Add the dressing and toss to coat. Serve the salad at once.

Apple & Date Coleslaw

INGREDIENTS

1 pear
1 red-skinned eating apple
225g/8oz red or white cabbage, or a mixture
3 carrots
200g/7oz can green flageolet beans, drained
50g/2oz/⅓ cup chopped dates
DRESSING
2.5ml/½ tsp dry English mustard
10ml/2 tsp clear honey
30ml/2 tbsp orange juice
5ml/1 tsp white wine vinegar
2.5ml/½ tsp paprika
salt and ground black pepper

SERVES 4–6

42

1 Make the dressing. In a small bowl, mix the mustard and honey until smooth. Add the orange juice, vinegar, paprika, salt and pepper to taste. Mix well.

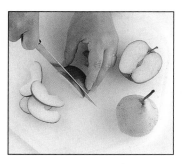

2 Cut the pear and apple into quarters, leaving the skin on. Remove the cores and slice the fruit thinly. Place in a bowl and toss with a little of the dressing.

3 Cut away the core from the cabbage. Shred the cabbage leaves very finely, discarding any other tough portions. Cut the carrots into very thin strips, about 5cm/2in long. Add the cabbage, carrots, flageolets and dates to the bowl. Mix well.

4 Pour over all the remaining dressing and toss thoroughly to coat. Cover the coleslaw and put in the fridge to chill for about 30 minutes before serving.

COOK'S TIP

Sultanas can be used instead of dates, if preferred. To plump them up, leave to marinate in the dressing for 15 minutes. Add the dressing and sultanas to the coleslaw and mix well.

Tomato & Feta Cheese Salad

INGREDIENTS

900g/2lb ripe tomatoes
200g/7oz feta cheese
120ml/4fl oz/½ cup extra virgin olive oil
12 black olives
ground black pepper
4 basil sprigs, to garnish (optional)

SERVES 4

1 Using a small, pointed knife cut around and then remove the tough cores from the tomatoes. Cut the tomatoes in thick slices and arrange in a shallow dish.

2 Crumble the feta cheese over the sliced tomatoes. Drizzle over the oil, add the olives and a grinding of black pepper. Garnish with the basil, if liked.

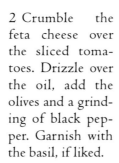

COOK'S TIP

It is traditional to use only olive oil when dressing tomato salads, but a dash of balsamic vinegar may be added to the oil if the tomatoes are particularly sweet, or if this is more to your taste.

Waldorf Ham Salad

INGREDIENTS

3 eating apples
15ml / 1 tbsp lemon juice
2 slices of cooked ham, about 175g / 6oz each
3 celery sticks
150ml / ¼ pint / ⅔ cup mayonnaise
½ bunch watercress, trimmed
1 escarole lettuce, separated into leaves
1 small radicchio lettuce, separated into leaves
45ml / 3 tbsp walnut oil or olive oil
50g / 2oz / ½ cup walnut pieces, toasted
salt and ground black pepper

SERVES 4

58

1 Quarter, peel and core the apples. Cut them into fine shreds, put in a bowl and toss with the lemon juice to prevent them turning brown.

2 Cut the ham and celery into 5cm / 2in strips and add to the apples. Spoon the mayonnaise over the apple, ham and celery mixture and toss to coat.

3 Slice the prepared escarole and radicchio lettuce leaves into fine shreds, put in a bowl and toss with the oil. Either set aside the watercress sprigs for garnishing or toss them with the lettuce now. Divide the dressed leaves among four plates.

4 Pile the mayonnaise mixture in the centre of each bed of leaves. Season with salt and pepper. Scatter the toasted walnuts on top and serve the salads at once, garnished with the watercress sprigs, if these have not yet been used.

Index